T̲h̲a̲n̲k YOU!

I want to thank God for trusting me with this assignment!

I want to thank my husband Pastor Troy
Bell (my Love) for believing in me in this
season and every season. You were one
of the first to believe in me and say
"Girl, Yes You Can!"

To my children that are still home:
Prosperity, Jasmin and T.J.
Thank you for allowing Mommy to focus
on my
Project many late afternoons. I
appreciate and honor your sacrifice!
Love you,
Eric (Britney), Julian and Jamin!

This is the Bell Tribe and after God
They are my first priority!

I love you guys.

"Girl, YES YOU CAN!"

To my Daughters, Natural and Spiritual
You are my reason why!

Prosperity, Jasmin, Britney
Catrina, Geneice, Stacey, Kamilah
Shonnece, Tracy and Alexis

And others who are yet to manifest,

Girl, Yes You can Do ALL things
Through Christ!

Sis, Put on Your Seatbelt! You are about to Break Down Walls!

Publisher's Note: This edition of "Girl, Yes You Can" is the first volume of several volumes. This is edition one of this Series.

"GIRL, YES YOU CAN"

A Journal / Daily Pick Me Up (Quotes) and Encouragement for Women of Purpose and Destiny.

ISBN-13: 9798591940072
Printed in the United States of America
©2021 by God's Butterflies Publishing

Contact: Katria Bell

katriabellbutterflies@gmail.com

Table of Contents

Stay Encouraged SIS!

Good morning, afternoon, or evening (depending on the time of day you are reading) my sister in Christ. I am so grateful that you are joining me in this conversation today and over next few days. I appreciate you buying or borrowing a copy of this book. It means the world to me that you decided to support me. I want to stress that this book will be written in the form of a conversation. This conversation is really from the heart of God to you. I am a woman who believes that God has brought me out of trauma to go and encourage and to help another woman up. I am an open vessel ready to help. My prayer for you is that something in this book would motivate you, help to validate you, and assist in cultivating your purpose. I pray that this book reminds you that you can do anything that God gives you the strength to do.

I was a woman that struggled with self-esteem and had a low self-image of who I was for many years. The visual of my purpose was distorted because of molestation and abuse as a child. I did not realize how I allowed the devastation of my childhood to hinder my ability to move forward in purpose and destiny. I portrayed confidence and a great sense of esteem on the outer appearance but within my inner self, there was a war going on! I fought this battle of low self-esteem daily and silently. I could easily portray that all was well to everyone around me, yet I knew that I did not honestly believe that I could live the God dreams that I saw prophetically as a girl. Could I really accomplish these grand visions and dreams God gave me?

I called that era of my life the "SILENT WAR"!! I screamed daily, internally, wishing that someone would hear me or at least render a clue, a supportive word, some reassurance that I could be all that God said I could. Could anyone see passed the mask, passed the make-believe costumes that I would wear daily? Yes, the enemy wanted to steal my ability to trust God, he wanted to steal my faith in God.

I have always asked God to give me the vision to see people for real. I wanted to see women passed what they portrayed. I celebrate how great you look! I give congratulations when you celebrate a small or large victory. I rejoice with you when you win or attain miracles and blessings. I clap when you sing, I shout when you overcome! However, I want to make sure that I see what God allows me to see passed the outer appearance. I am not so impressed by the outer. I celebrate the outer, but I take the time to look towards the inner woman. I want to be available to take a deeper look just in case God needs me to.

I realized, after years of my own struggle, that many people are secretly crying out for help and wishing that someone, anyone would refuse to believe what is being shown. It was exhausting to keep up the "everything is ok" mode. God marked me for greatness and there was warfare sent to derail me from fulfilling my purpose. This war included the internal dialogue that many of us have within ourselves. That dialogue that questions if we are truly equipped, smart enough, pretty enough, tall enough, rich enough to complete the assignment. I was so tired, and I needed help. I was bleeding and I needed help. I am here to burst the myth right now that you are less powerful if you admit that you do not have it all together. Sis, if you need help, it is ok to be honest about not being ok. If you are having an off day, it is ok. If you are ok, then that is ok too. If you have moved past your trauma and are living your best life, I celebrate you today! Whatever place you are in right now, just know that it is ok and that you will be ok. God still has a plan for you, and you are well on your way. I am so, so excited! Girl, you can rise above the internal war. Remember you are more than a conqueror. You are an overcomer. Girl, yes you can!

Listen, I may not be talking to every woman that picks up this book, but I know that I am speaking to some women that will need this conversation. If this book is not for you that is ok too, but may I ask a favor of you? Please give it to a woman that you know needs to hear a word of encouragement in this area. Give it to a woman who is struggling and needs a bit of light at the end of her tunnel. Give it to a woman who you support, a woman or girl you want to fan the flame of her fire to keep her ignited.

The heart of this book is to break the cycle and the stigma that women cannot work alongside one another and support one another. I want to help break generational cycles of cattiness, of jealousy and pettiness. I want to help feed the narrative that Kingdom women in ministry, the marketplace, in education, in politics, and in every area of society can come together in unity. I once heard a quote that, "true queens can fix another woman's crown when it's crooked without telling someone else that you did". This is true sisterhood. I want to see you succeed, I want to see you live your best life and I want to help you get there by being in your fan club and rooting you on from the side-lines. I do not want to steal your light or shine when it is your turn to shine. I want to whole-heartedly rejoice for your successes and to celebrate your victories.

Too many women are giving up on their families and their marriages, their dreams, goals and visions and it is time to step up to push another woman. Too many women are coping with addictions and depression alone. Too many women are contemplating and have committed suicide because someone did not take out the time to say "Girl, yes you can do this!!" I know my assignment for you today. I know my assignment for this book. I pray that this conversation will bring some light and some encouragement to some dark places in Jesus' name.

If no one has told you today, Sis I love you and I do not have to know you! I want you to know that someone is praying for you and rooting for you. Yes, I am praying for you while typing the words to this book. I knew you would need to pick up this book with a bit of hope and light.

You are not alone, and you are about to show this world who God made you to be. This is your time, this is your season, sis this is your year. You do not have to do this alone. Your destiny is in your hands. God has already marked you. You were born and created because of your purpose. Your destiny is awaiting your YES. There is power in your words and today I speak life over you. Some areas in your life have been dry for a long, long time and no one has come by with the water of the spirit to saturate your dry areas. Well, here is some water today God's Princess, Queen of your castle it is time to drink.

I decree and declare that this will be the boost and launching pad that you need to get up and set your world ablaze. There is a world out here waiting on you. We are waiting on you and the season of despair and stagnation is over. I begin by encouraging you and speaking God's plan and goodness over your life, and then you must begin to speak life over your destiny. You are worth it, and I cannot wait to see how you shake hell in this season.

Come on warrior, we are some girls who are about to find out who we are. This is "GIRL POWER" for real Kingdom style. We are women on a mission, and we are not playing any more games. We are tired of being defeated and depressed. No longer victims and no longer victimized. We choose to be victors today!! It is our time; it is our year, and we are about to take center stage in Jesus' name. Let's GO!!

Your Kingdom Assignment

What is a Kingdom? A kingdom is a country, state, or territory ruled by a king or queen. Where are all the Queens? However, we understand as children of God we reference Kingdom in the realm of God's rule and reign as the authority of God. The word kingdom in laymen's terms is Gods' way of doing things. We as believers know that we are in the earth realm to establish God's kingdom in the earth. Matthew (6:10) reads, "your will be done on earth as it is in heaven." The part you play in God's great plan is to establish Kingdom wherever He sends you.

It can be difficult to understand this weighty concept. To accomplish this instruction in the earth you must understand your authority. Woman of God, before you read one quote in this book your baseline understanding will have to be that you carry the authorized power of heaven to facilitate actions on behalf of God. Wait a minute and let that sink in. You have been endowed with power from heaven to bid heaven's plan, government and, to accomplish heaven's assignments in the earth. You are an ambassador of Heaven (God's Kingdom). Sis, you are powerful in God. Understand your authority.

As a parent I do not ask my children permission to watch tv, or to leave my house when I need to take care of business, that sounds backwards doesn't it? I understand my position as mom. I automatically carry authority in my home to establish order, structure, safety and provision for my children. You do not need to wait another day for permission. Your marching orders come from God. Yes, we wait on the timing of God and the instruction of the Lord, but you have been deputized.

I am here to just remind you that you already carry the authority to carry out your God- given assignment. Too many of you have been living beneath your purpose. Rise Kingdom Women and GO live on purpose!

Genesis 1:28 says in part, "and God said unto them, Be fruitful, and multiply, and replenish the earth, and subdue it, and have dominion...."

Dominion, dominion, dominion, dominion is such a word of rank and authority. There is nothing about the word dominion that should cause you to shrink, duck or hide. As believers we must believe what God says about us, and we must carry out the full intent and instruction of what the word gives to us. This is a reminder to some and an introduction of thought to others that you have been called to dominate and subdue. Subdue defined is to bring (a country or people) under control by force. We are called to take this world by force for God's Kingdom.

Katria, why are you beginning this book writing about dominion, authority and subduing? I am glad you asked woman of God. I want to remind you of your beginning in God. Remember you were created because of God's love for you and to accomplish your purpose. You will not accomplish purpose in the earth and effectively execute your purpose unless you understand your weight in the earth. I believe that many people have not accomplished purpose in the earth because they do not understand that THEY CAN! Listen, YOU CAN, because GOD SAID SO! Mothers, we know what that means right? If you asked God, "is it possible to do all that you have called me to do? God answers, "yes, and you respond, why? His response would be, "because I said you could daughter, it is in my word that you can do all things through me".

You do not need to wait for approval to JUMP. You do not need permission from anyone in this earth to LEAP into purpose.

LEAP!!!

I speak directly into your spirit today to remember who you are. If you do not really understand who you are, please go pick up your bible and begin to read what it says concerning you.

It is not that we do not have what it takes to accomplish the will of the father. We become our own stumbling blocks in purpose. Some of you know what God says about you, but you do not quite believe it. That is the purpose of this book. I will encourage you in your thinking and I will help you in practical application, however this book is to remind you that you already have what it takes to accomplish your kingdom assignment. What would your husband or children think if you were to ask me permission to enter your own house when you have the keys in your hand? Your family would probably say, "Mom, what are you doing? You have the keys, just open the door. Are you ok? Just go into the house." In God's sovereign love, He is saying the same to you today. What are you doing daughter? You already have the orders in your hand; go handle your business. What are you waiting on? Your presence in the earth is reason enough that you should be about the business of the Father, because "Girl, You CAN! This is heaven's authority that has been rendered to you. What power or person on earth has arms long enough to box with God? Not one in the earth trumps the authority that you have been given.

This is just a little reminder that God's placement of you in the earth gives you the authority to move and just LIVE ON PURPOSE! So, get up and LIVE!

Now, let us begin our conversation together sis. You have a life to live on today and every day of your assignment. It is time to RISE, KINGDOM WOMAN, because "YOU CAN".

CHAPTER

1

I CAN'T WEAR THEIR ARMOR. IT DOESN'T FIT!

No longer will I try to fit into something that doesn't fit me. I can only wear a custom design. Tailor Made BABY!

#1

"I Can't Wear Your Armor, It Doesn't Fit!"

Good morning Woman of God, you are at the beginning of another day, why not live it on purpose? If there is still breath in your lungs, then we need what you have. Someone's life is depending on your "yes" today. Live out loud and on purpose and in purpose. Go ahead, begin your day with a "Yes" to God.

Today's quote is so important to your authenticity. We need more authentic women to represent Kingdom and to represent our families and cultures. It is so easy to get caught up in what society says you should be, who your family says you should become, and all the boxes that people try to lock you into. It is time to break this mold. Get out of that darn box, TODAY! Did you hear me Daughter of God? BREAK OUT! Aren't you tired of being hymned in, boxed up in limitations? Limitations like putting on a size 8 ½ shoe when you know you wear a 10, you are asking for trouble right?

It has become a lost art to embrace who God created you to be. There is so much pressure in this world, especially among women to become what the world says is the "It Factor". The world's comparison between women is nauseating. It is painful to see women who try to be everything but authentic. We need your flavor, your color, your personality, your flare, your anointing, your style. We need and want to see it all! There is beauty in originality! Take off "their" shoes, they do not fit anyway.

The pressure to become someone great in today's climate can be tiresome. Our world is saturated with likes, hearts, follows, shares, and comments on all social media platforms, which produces a false sense of accomplishment. Why should our value be based on the accolades and praises of people that we do not even know? At the end of the day if people do not like you now, then fasten your seatbelt, the haters will surely show up when you truly walk into your authenticity. However, your focus should be on those that God has sent to push you, and who will hold you accountable to your original design. I need women, in my life, who will not allow me to settle for less than God's very best for me.

So many of our sisters are walking around with costumes and masks on because someone told them that it was the best fit for them. It is like putting on someone's hand-me downs, when there is a tailor-made purpose waiting for you.

I Samuel 17:38-40 reads:

*"**38** So Saul clothed David with his [a]armor, and he put a bronze helmet on his head; he also clothed him with a coat of mail. **39** David fastened his sword to his armor and tried to walk, for he had not tested them. And David said to Saul, "I cannot walk with these, for I have not tested them." So, David took them off.*

***40** Then he took his staff in his hand; and he chose for himself five smooth stones from the brook, and put them in a shepherd's bag, in a pouch which he had, and his sling was in his hand. And he drew near to the Philistine.*

In this scripture, King Saul did his best to help David prepare for this battle. Sidenote: Everyone who tries to give advice to help you is not out to harm you. Some people try to help in the only way that they know-how. However, David was confident enough in his call and anointing to know who he was and what he carried. He remembered how God trained him with the bear, and he was comfortable in his own skin. He remembered his anointing and was bold enough to show up with what he had been given. David was an original that day just like every other day. I love this story because David was confident enough to take off the fancy armour and he showed up to the fight with his slingshot and 5 smooth stones. My God, that is a word right there! Are you strong enough, confident enough, bold enough to show up with what you have been given? What David had was all that he needed. WOW, I feel that today. At times, we find ourselves asking God for something else because we feel that we do not have enough. I hear God today, and He says you have all that you need right now. Take what you have and start! YOU ARE ENOUGH!

The word for you today is to be confident in what God has given you for your purpose. You may be thinking, am I enough? You may have witnessed what works for others, and God says for you today, you must do it the way He designed for you. Remember, you have all you need. What He gave you is sufficient! God has a specific plan just for you.

I want to encourage you today that you are enough. The world needs your flavour, your anointing, your purpose, your call and your personality. Those that are waiting on you need what "YOU" have right now!

Do not wait on perfection. Hey sis, you can start today with what you have? Look at your hands, look in your closet, look in your attic, look in your journal, look in your heart and explore what you have been given.

Give yourself permission today to take off every mask, costume, and every piece of armour that does not fit. Be honest, you have been frustrated trying to wear something that was not designed for you. You are drained because it is too heavy, and you cannot move with all the extra weight.

You can do more with what seems like a little. Girl, Yes you can!! I am so excited about your next season. There is a fresh wind blowing now over your decision today. You are about to sense a refreshing and experience a season of restoration over your mind as you go back to the basics to work with what God gave you!

What do you need to take off today? What extra weight do you need to take off? Write it down now. Faith without works is dead. Do it now! Permit yourself right now. Do not wait.

Today I take off....

_____
_____
_____
_____
_____
_____
_____
_____

......These things no longer belong to me. I permit myself to operate in my authentic purpose and destiny without the need to explain my actions to anyone. I continue to submit to your will God, and I acknowledge you in all my ways Lord.

Take out the moment to breathe in and out. Breathe in the refreshing of the Lord and exhale the extra weight. Release yourself from the expectations of other people. Wow, you are headed somewhere great, and it starts right now on TODAY!! Let's GO!

Action Plan......

Every day for a week, make it a point to recognize those things that you have picked up that are not authentically you. When you recognize the habits, patterns, thoughts etc. write them down and then say out loud this is not me. Journal your thoughts below:

_____
_____
_____
_____
_____
_____
_____
_____
_____
_____
_____
_____
_____
_____
_____
_____
_____
_____
_____

CHAPTER

2

IT'S NEVER TOO LATE TO BEGIN!

I don't care how old you are or
how many times you've tried.
Sis, it's never too late to begin!
LET'S GO!

#2

"It's never too late to Begin!"

Good morning Queens! I want you to wake up every day with a refreshing word to remind you of who you are. Can you get up today and live on purpose? My answer is always, "GIRL, YES YOU CAN DO THIS!! Before you complete this book, you will not be asking, "Can I do this", you will be asking God, ok how do I, and when do I and what time can I do this! Girls we are on a roll, let's go!!

Stop telling yourself that you are too old and too late in life to start again. I do not care if you are 96 years old, there is something in your life left to accomplish. We have all lived with should of, would of, and could of thoughts in our lives. Those would-of statements are just excuses keeping you stagnant from progressing towards destiny. Stop excusing yourself and live on purpose! Did you hear me sis? No more excuses. An excuse is just that, an excuse. Do not embrace any more justifications of why you cannot finish what you started. Where there is a will then there is a way. I decree a finisher's anointing over you on today and in this season.

The famous designer Vera Wang did not design her first dress until she was 40 years old. This woman was a professional ice skater for years and dared to step out of her comfort zone. What if she would have let her age give her an excuse? Honey, I would not be wearing my Vera Wang dresses today. Yes, Vera!! Thank you for entering our world and daring to do something different.

Henry Ford was 45 years old when he created the Model T car in 1908. Thank God for Henry, because of his innovation we are driving in style now ladies! Do you see where I am going women of purpose? Oh, trust me I am coming for you today.

Samuel L Jackson was 43 before he hit it big in his first award-winning film in Spike Lee's Jungle Fever. Yes, the actor Samuel Jackson had performed in a few films before he hit the big one. He did not quit, he kept going and now Mr. Jackson is everywhere. Doesn't it seem like he is in all the movies? LOL! Ok back to my point.

Sam Walton was a semi-successful retail store owner in his 20's and 30's however his success was defined and skyrocketed in his 40's when he opened the first Walmart store in Rogers, Arkansas. Now we all shop at Walmart. Thank God for Walmart. Can I get an amen ladies? I will say it, AMEN!

The famous chef and cook extraordinaire Julia Childs did not launch her first cookbook until age 50 and became a tv food sensation to her foodie fans. Where are my foodies at?

The powerful Christian speaker Joyce Meyer didn't get her big break until her mid 40's after 5 years of doing a home bible study for 13-30 people faithfully. This is one of my favorite stories. I love her story and I love how she beat the odds. This woman had every reason not to try. Years of being raped and molested by her biological father and living with a mother who knew about the abuse but did not save her from her abusive husband or the trauma and heartbreak.

Joyce did not stop, she could not help what happened her, but she chose what she became and because of it my life was changed. She is still reaching millions of women across the globe because she believed that she could do what God called her to do despite her trauma!

Anna Mary Robertson Moses started a painting career at the graceful age of 76 years old. She sold one of her paintings for 1.2 million dollars. Who said that age had to stop you from living your dreams? You better go on Anna Mary Robertson. Madame Robertson became rich at a seasoned age! It is never too late ladies.

My point is, what if all these people allowed their age, their failures or traumatic experiences to become their reasons for not following through with their God-given talent and gifts? Our world would not be the same if they had not plowed through the same negative thoughts that every human battles. If they had not overcome, then this world would not have experienced the treasures that were on the inside of each of them.

This word is for you today. I do not care how many times you have failed or how long you may have had to wait. It is your time to get up and begin today. Do not wait, JUST DO IT NOW!

This is the pre-mediated attack of the enemy to launch this negative pattern of delay in your life. He loves to tell you, "That you have waited too long or that it's too late for you." He says, "You might as well give up now." We dismantle the lie right now in the name of Jesus and we break that stronghold from your mind now. Let us pray now.

Lord, I thank you for my sister who is reading this book right now. We thank you that according to Jeremiah 29:11, For I know the plans I have for you," declares the LORD, "plans to prosper you and not to harm you, plans to give you hope and a future.
I thank you, Lord, for my sister's bright, prosperous future. You have the best in store for her and I pray that she receives your absolute best for her right now. It is never too late to begin this journey of purpose and I thank you Lord that you are going before her to make every path straight and clear for her arrival. It is never too late; you just need her to agree and to move in faith. Say this sis....... This is my year! This is my day! In Jesus' name.

Action Plan

Now we are Women on purpose, right? So, we never just speak but we also move on what we believe! What is your plan for today? Make your to-do list right now and follow through. Make a realistic plan and check it off as you go.

1. _____
2. _____
3. _____
4. _____
5. _____

Hey, I am proud of you. You are about to impact this world in such an amazing way. Way to go! I cannot wait to hear of the wonderful results of your moves on today. It just takes one decision to change the trajectory of your life.

CHAPTER

3

KEEP WALKING SIS, YOU ARE GETTING THERE!

YOU are gaining more
ground than you Realize,
Keep Moving!

#3

"Keep Walking Sis, You are Getting There! You are gaining more ground than you Realize, Keep Moving!"

It is another day Princess, and you are alive which means you have a purpose to fulfill today! I am so excited for you. Go ahead and do your make up today. Put on that new pair of earrings. Wear that new pair of shoes or that hat you have been waiting for a special occasion to wear, go ahead and put it on today. You are the occasion SIS! Can you do it? "GIRL, YES YOU CAN! Let's Go!

I want to encourage you to keep pushing today. Ladies, we work hard! I can see your heads shaking up and down now in agreement. Ladies we are professionals, moms, wives, caregivers, pastors, business owners, and so much more. We work hard! No matter what we do we go hard and give everything we must to take care of what is important to us. Women today are working hard to pay the bills and to put food on the table because it is necessary. Many women are doing much of this without a support system. I am sending a shout out to all the single mothers out there right now. Can we take a moment and send up a prayer for every single mother doing it on her own! You are not alone sis, and I pray at this moment that God would send His love to you and a supernatural blessing for your house for holding it down for your babies. It can become discouraging to go to work and to pick up the kids, make a grocery run, make dinner, watch a bit of TV and go to bed, just to get up and do it all over again.

To even think about fulfilling a dream outside of work hours is exhausting. I send encouragement and the strength of the Lord to all the wives, mothers, single women who go to work, come home to cook dinner, then to pick up kids before dashing to the grocery store, helping with homework in the car, while you are going to school yourself and building a business while taking care of momma and other family members! We must give God the glory ladies. God gives us a strength that could only come from Him. Women are truly superheroes! All glory goes to God. Seasons of investing into your future will pay off. I know you may be tired but keep going my sister. You are gaining ground. Keep burning the midnight oil to accomplish your dream. Let me encourage you, it will be worth it. Do not stop, your labor is not in vain.

When building a dream from the ground up, the construction site can look messy. Sometimes obstacles, issues, finances, people, and even our thoughts can question our reason for attempting such extraordinary tasks? We begin to ask ourselves, "Am I crazy to believe that I can become a self-employed business owner? I barely have time to take a shower and look in the mirror. Can I finish my degree and go on to obtain my Master's? Can I become a career woman and still be a mother and a wife? Do I have what it takes to become a minister of the gospel and minister to hurting people when I am a wreck? These questions and more can arise when you are breaking the normal routines of life to conquer the other side of the "WHAT IF.... You fill in the blank. Can you do all this Powerhouse? What Is our answer? "GIRL, YES YOU CAN!!"

This quote today is to remind you that faithfulness and hard work does eventually yield a harvest. You are getting close to where you want to be. I know you are tired sis, but do not give up. I know it seems like you are so far behind in this race but keep running! Your second and third and fourth wind are blowing your way now in Jesus' name!

I know when you began last time that circumstances knocked you down, but you found your way back up. You were knocked down but not knocked out. You have a super-natural help which is God. I pray the Holy Spirit's empowerment over you right now. OOOOHHH, I feel that wind of heaven blowing your way right now. Receive that sis!

Zechariah 4:10 says- Do not despise small beginnings for the Lord rejoices to see the work begin…….

There is something to be said about "Your Start". I want to know, are you farther along than you were when you started? If your answer is yes and you can see movement, then I am here to celebrate with you. You might say, but I only have one side of the dream built, well I say, "Let's admire your amazing wall!!" Come on, perspective is everything! Is it more than what was built last year? Then we have something to celebrate.

If you have not started, then remember it is never too late to begin. Get up and make some moves today!

Action Plan

I want you to write down your successes in the last year. What can you celebrate? I want you to write it down, even if you consider it a small victory. I know in seasons of building you may not have many fans or much of a support system. So, if I may, let me sign up to become a member of your fan club today. I would like to say that "I am so proud of your "WALL." I can see where you are going with this building, and I cannot wait to see the finished product!" Please tell me more, what have you accomplished? Email me at katriabellministries@gmail.com and share with me your testimony and send me your Facebook name and your website information. I want to support you. Yes, I am for real, let me celebrate with you. Oh, you all thought I was playing. I want to pray with you and celebrate with you. I am signing up for your fan club today. Email me and write down your milestones in this book!

1._____
2._____
3._____
4._____
5._____

Father, I thank you for my friend here today that may need a little encouragement and cheers for their small successes. You see her heart and her hard work and God you are pleased when we step out in faith to believe outside of the box. God, you made her to do extraordinary things in this world. I thank you that you begin to show my sister how far she has come and remind her that her future is attainable.

I thank you that we can do all things through Christ that strengthens us according to Philippians 4:13. Thank you for your love and your support, because at the end of the day you are still our biggest supporter!

Continue to write out your accomplishments and do something today to celebrate your feats. Go treat yourself to a cup of coffee or even a new dress or purse.

Come on girl, you deserve it. Congratulations, sis and remember to keep building. I will read your email. Send it.

_____
_____
_____
_____
_____
_____
_____
_____
_____
_____
_____
_____
_____
_____
_____
_____
_____
_____
_____
_____
_____
_____
_____

CHAPTER

4

STOP, WAITING ON THEM TO UNDERSTAND YOUR MOVEMENT.....

Be about the Father's
Business. They will
understand you Later!

#4

"Stop waiting on "THEM" to Understand Your Movement, Be about the Father's Business. They will understand you Later!"

Hello dynamic woman, you are beginning a new day! Are you excited? If not, go ahead and pump yourself up, encourage yourself in the Lord. If yesterday was a bad day, then I pray that God would give you the strength to look up today. Hold your head up and expect God to bring miracles. Expect God to bring you into your good land today! We look to the hills from where our help comes from because our help comes from the Lord. Psalms 121

This quote can be a difficult one to live through. As humans, it is natural to want acceptance, validation, and approval by those that are important to us. It is a part of our need for human interaction and affection from others. It does not matter how hard your outer shell is and how much you may not think you need people, God made us to need one another. You need someone. I need someone! The way you respond to that need is crucial to how you move forward towards your purpose. You can want approval from people, but it is not necessary. I have lost years waiting for people to understand what God gave me to do. I once heard a man of God say," it was not a conference call when God delivered your message of purpose". It was a one-way conversation between you and God. It is okay for people to question your direction and your movement, but it is not okay that you stop moving because of it.

When you are called to do something that is extraordinary, your actions may present questions from those that are around you. I have learned that everyone is not against me, and people's hearts are not always set to stop me or intended to hurt me. People's faith level may not be at the level that your faith is and that is ok, really it is ok. God gave you the vision and the dream, so you can see where you are going. God did not show them your vision, or your goals so no need to be disappointed when people cannot see your path.

During this season of building, be careful of who you reveal your dreams to. You cannot expose your dreams to everyone. It is so important to have like-minded people around you that understand your extreme leaps of faith, especially when you are called to operate in unknown realms. When you have a pioneering or trailblazer anointing, you need people that understand "extreme" moves. Have people that understand your plight and who will believe God with you. Those that will hold you accountable and those that will cover you. My Apostle calls these people your "consecrated counsel".

Being a pioneer of new territories is already scary enough, and you need people around you who can encourage you on your journey even when you seem outrageous in your actions. If you have people around you that misunderstand you, keep it moving, you do not stop because of their misunderstanding. Do not allow their confusion or lack of understanding to derail you off your path. You must remain focused during this season. Time is of the essence.

GIRL, YES YOU CAN!!!

Transparent moment, I have wasted precious hours and days, because I became inundated with everyone else's concerns about my destiny. Sounds ridiculous when I say it out loud. I was literally sitting around waiting for everyone's approval as if my purpose were determined by "them". God did not invite everyone in on the "CALL" of my life. The select few that He did invite, they could understand where I was going and they are there to protect, cultivate and to push me to where God was taking me.

I encourage you to stop waiting. Some of you are waiting on your haters, enemies and even family to GET IT! It is an extremely hard pill to swallow, but some of those people may never get it. Does that excuse you from your destiny? NO! Can you still accomplish your destiny without people getting it? Girl, Yes You Can! Say it with me, (YOUR NAME), Yes you CAN! We will repeat and rehearse this line until you believe it. The bible says that "The gifts and callings of God are without repentance", Romans 11:29. He gave you your gifts unapologetically which means you get to fulfill your purpose unapologetically. No need to explain yourself, you are approved!

The reality is that some people will never understand you or even appreciate you until after you have accomplished your goal. It is like never being invited to the table until someone else, somewhere else, invites you, then suddenly you are acknowledged and invited to the table. That is ok too sis, there will always be those that overlook you but do not stop soaring. Get up and shine.

Amos 3:3 King James Version
Can two walk together, except they be agreed?

36

This scripture is so powerful. We can find ourselves frustrated because we are trying to walk with those that are not in agreement with us. People that are not aligned or equally yoked with you can cause issues and interference. Acknowledge what level you are called to and surround yourself with those that are at least on that level or even greater. I am not saying to throw away people that do not understand your plight; what I am saying is to not expect everyone to understand where you are going. You may have to leave some behind, and that is ok too! Girl, find your tribe. Understand right now who you can have a conversation with concerning your future. Everyone in your life should not have privy to that part of you. Only those who are vetted, tried and true should be in that consecrated space with you. That valuable part of you is set aside only for those who can pray with you, see where you are going, cultivate an atmosphere of faith, those that will push you, love you and keep you accountable when you want to give up. I am speaking about those who have been tested in the fire of challenges and are found to still be standing when it is all over. These are the people you talk to and lean on! Surround yourself with people that have purposes of their own and are living their lives in motion.

Sis do not sit around any longer and cry over who will not ever get you! My dear sister you have so much work to do. Haven't you wasted enough mental energy and tears over this? Can you do this without them understanding you? GIRL, OF COURSE YOU CAN!!

Lord, I pray over my sister today and I declare that No weapon formed against her will be able to prosper according to Isaiah 54:17. We tear down the weapons of rejection, abandonment, confusion, mis-understanding and interference now in the mighty name of Jesus! She is more than a conqueror according to Romans 8:37 and she will accomplish more in this season than she ever has before. She will no longer wait on approval, but she will pursue in the name of Jesus.

Action Plan

Alright ladies, you know we do not just talk about purpose, but we are about action after the conversation. Re-evaluate who is in your circle, write down the names of those they you may need to move into another space. This is your personal book so please be honest with yourself.

1. _____
2. _____
3. _____
4. _____
5. _____

Now add some names of those that you need to communicate with and even those you need to seek out to engage with. Do not be afraid. GO FOR IT!!!

1. _____
2. _____
3. _____

CHAPTER

5

STOP! GO BACK AND FINISH WHAT YOU STARTED

You are not a quitter. You can do this!

#5
"Stop! Go back and finish what you started. You are not a quitter. You can do this!"

Hello Victorious One, how are you today? I pray that you are waking up every day just waiting to get started on your journey towards your destiny. Remember there is a world waiting on you Lady!! You are so full of dormant potential and purpose, and I decree and declare that you will not leave this earth with all of that "GOLD" on the inside of you. We need you to be active sis, let's go!

Today's quote is somewhat of an encouragement and directive. I want to take a moment to send a firm word of encouragement your way, wrapped in the love of God.

I am asking you to take some time today and make a list of all the unfinished projects that you have started in the last year and have not completed. It does not matter how small the project is, jot it down and make a list. Some examples of unfinished projects may include cleaning the closet, organizing the garage, writing the business idea (plan), or paying off your credit card debt in order to purchase a home. Whatever the project is write it down right now. We are about to look at where you are located along with executing a plan to finish. You are about to break the cycle of procrastination and enter a season of finishing what you have started, but only if you are willing. You can skip over this section if you want, however, those women that are serious, take the time to sit, think and write down these projects right now. Let's work ladies.

Unfinished Projects

1._____

2._____

3._____

4._____

5._____

6._____

7._____

8._____

9._____

10._____

11._____

12._____

If you need another sheet of paper, go ahead and keep writing until you have jotted down every unfinished project.

This year, this month, today you are about to become a finisher!

Now when you have completed the list, take and prioritize them from easiest task (quicker to complete) to most difficult task (longest to complete). I know this seems taxing, unimportant, and maybe even a waste of time, but trust me some of the smallest, practical inconsistencies in our lives can keep you revolving around the same mountains. This happens simply because of the lack of discipline to obey the small thing that God asked us to do.

The scripture says in:

M a t t h e w   2 5 : 2 1

"His lord said unto him, Well done, THOU good and faithful servant: thou hast been faithful over a few things, I will make thee ruler over many things: enter thou into the joy of thy lord.

We would rather keep asking God what is my next assignment? God, please show me the path to my next season. Why am I still stuck God? Where is my energy? Why am I drained and lacking motivation? Maybe your next instruction or promotion was connected to your obedience in the last instruction from God. It is extremely easy to ignore the last directive trying to get to the next place, but God was using it as a test to see if you could follow his plan to be obedient. The completion of the last assignment would have promoted you to the next level. It is like trying to go to college without first receiving your high school diploma.

Let's go in order of importance, list your items.

1.   6.

2.   7.

3.   8.

4.   9.

5.   10.

This chapter is not about getting you to do busywork. This chapter is to activate you for your next season sis. This chapter is about obedience to the last instruction that you were given. You may ask, now how is cleaning my closet going to help me reach the community that I am called to?

Well, the discipline to clean the closet, keep it clean, and organize it will forge in you a consistency of organization and order that will ultimately bleed over in your work ethic and the way you deal with people. Many times, we think that our public life will not eventually reveal our lack of attention to the details in our personal lives. This is how the CEO of a Fortune 500 company, or the Pastor of a Mega Church falls from grace or is eventually caught in fraudulent activities. They never took the time to get rid of the small foxes that eventually spoil the vine. Have you heard of the old saying "It's the small rot that kills?" At some point, we are all allowed an opportunity to allow God to sharpen us and to develop and cultivate character traits and integrity that will sustain us on the mountain top. But it is up to us to pay attention to these areas and to work them into greatness.

The bible reads in Matthew 25:23 that if we are faithful over a few things, that God would make us ruler over many things. I will encourage you today my sister to go ahead finish what you started. Bear down and just get it done. There is a lesson that must be learned. You must have the last instruction complete before you get to your next door of opportunity. Many of you will get your next instruction while obeying this one!! My God today. Let's Go.

Lord, I thank you that today we have a willing and obedient spirit to go back and finish the last instruction that you gave us. We will no longer ignore your unction and nudge that you quietly whisper, "to pick it back up and complete it". You are looking for those that will obey you. We will obey! Please forgive us for ignoring your instructions and for minimizing the task in our minds. We want to please you, and we thank you for your wisdom and guidance on how to get back on track. We thank you for your love and being the God of 2nd chances!!

Action Plan

Your action plan today is simple. Make a quick, realistic timeline on when you will complete each task.

_____
_____
_____
_____
_____
_____
_____
_____
_____
_____

CHAPTER

6

HAVE THE AUDACITY TO BELIEVE WHAT GOD SAYS ABOUT YOU!

Lord,
Remove my
unbelief!

#6
"Have the Audacity to Believe what God says about YOU! Lord, Remove my Unbelief."

Good morning Warrior Woman! You are a fighter, and I am proud of you for fighting and pursuing destiny. Yes, you sis! Are you still here? Did the last fight kill you? Are you still striving for greater? Then you are a warrior. Sometimes the greatest sign of fighting is to get up today to just keep moving. This life is not easy and if you told your story queen, then the world would see why you are a walking miracle. You are God's daughter, and you are to be celebrated! Thank you for fighting. We need you.

Today's quote is so especially important to me. This one took me years to grasp. I am a 44-year-old woman and I have just whole-heartedly embraced totally who God says I am in the last few years of my life. I believe that one of the greatest tactics of the enemy is to keep us ignorant of our authority and power in this earth realm. If he keeps us from knowing who we are and how much power lies on the inside of us, then he can keep the Kingdom of God from advancing and he can then keep you from your purpose and operating in your jurisdiction to evoke change in people's lives.

It takes a bold and courageous woman to believe God past her faults, flaws, and issues. Let's not even talk about traumas, loss, abuse, abandonment, rejection, and how all of that affect us. Those are additional obstacles that many of us fight daily to get past. But this is a fight that you must engage in.

Today, I speak to the warrior on the inside of you! There is one on the inside of each of us. What if someone were to try to harm one of your children or someone that you love? I wonder what will happen to that uninformed person? I do not have to wonder because the warrior in you would rise and deal with that threat! No questions asked, it would be handled! Am I right or am I wrong? The intuitive nature of a fighter was woven into our being. God knew that we would need it. We use it for survival and protection.

However, the enemy uses attacks, trauma, and discouragement to wear you down. After years and years of betrayals and people turning on you and life just coming at you one-thousand miles per hour, eventually, you are worn out! That is the plan of the enemy to restructure and rename your identity. He then calls you damaged goods. The enemy is the accuser of the brethren according to Revelation 12:10. This devil not only accuses you but then he wants to call you the cheater, the liar, the used up has- been. He calls us everything but a daughter of God. If that was not bad enough then he will use people to reinforce that narrative and speak the same poison into your ears that then filter directly into your spirit.

Before you know it, you are then believing the story that the enemy has painted and that is when you begin to live out the seeds of death that the enemy has planted into your spirit and soul. The bible says that "Whatsoever a man thinketh in his heart so is he" Proverbs 23:6-8.

What do you think of yourself today? What thoughts or ideas have you reinforced into your heart and mind?

Let's do our daily exercise. Go to a mirror right now if you have one near you. Speak out what you see. Speak out loud what you say to yourself quietly. What are the statements that you repeat over and over in your mind?

Are they purposeful, uplifting, building thoughts? Or do you immediately see what someone said about you? Do you see an unworthy woman? Or do you see a supernatural survivor? Do you see a victim or are you looking at a victor? My sister, God's daughter, your perspective is everything. Yes, molestation happened to me, but I refuse to let it control me. It happened but it will not dictate my future. I control now where I go and what I do in the plan of God. You cannot help what people will say and what they remember or even what those people did to you. You cannot help what happened to you but sis you sure can do something about it now. We have given people too much authority over our lives, and many of them are going on living their own lives or have died and you are still giving them your power.

Take back your authority and begin to speak life back into dead places in your life. Today we speak nothing but the word over you. Death and life are in the power of the tongue, so use your power to speak life right now.

Action Plan

I want you to grab 3 scriptures to speak over yourself to build yourself. Oh, I could do it for you, but it would not mean as much. You know your voids and deficiencies. You know what you need and most importantly God knows what you need. I just pray right now that the Holy Spirit would quicken your spirit and give you the words needed today. Please take the time to write out your three scriptures and then speak them over yourself at least three times.

Scripture # 1

Scripture #2

Scripture #3

Today, you deserve a fresh wind of life and restoration. Speak to yourself, encourage yourself, sis. Do not wait on anyone else to do it for you. Get your boldness back and take your authority back. Get the audacity to go back to what God says about you and say it until you believe it. Get in that mirror every day and speak scriptures over yourself. There is still life and power in God's word. Give yourself an opportunity to receive a fresh drink of living water on today. It has been said that we believe 80% of what we say. So, get started, Warrior. This is how I fight my battles today by speaking nothing but life over myself. Old thoughts and negative seeds must be uprooted in Jesus' name.

Come on sis, let's go!! You have got this.

CHAPTER

7

LET THEM LAUGH, WORK YOUR FAITH, OBEY GOD

They laughed at Noah (ark) too, Who profited in the end?

#7
"Let them laugh, Work your faith, Obey God! They laughed at Noah (ark) too, Who profited in the end?"

Good morning Purposed Woman. Are you ready for today? Are you excited to live your dreams, to live your purpose? If you are not excited, then I encourage you to get excited. There is so much purpose yet to be revealed and lived. You can live your dreams. Girl, yes, you can do this!!

I want to quote Theodore Roosevelt:

"It is not the critic who counts; not who points out how the strong man stumbles....... The credit belongs to the man in the arena....

It is so easy for some people to sit and laugh at someone else's efforts. It seems so easy because they are not the ones doing the work. When God gives you an assignment, everyone will not understand your moves and your reason why. I used to question God why is it that people could not see what I saw, especially being a woman with a prophetic eye and voice. I had to eventually understand that everyone is not supposed to see what I see. Everyone is not supposed to understand what God told me to do. That conversation is between me and God.

I finally accepted that you may never understand me or support me. If you see it or understand it then great, however, if you do not, that is ok as well. Too many times we allow the chatter of those on the sidelines to halt our progress and that day is over Queen!

There will always be critics chattering. There will always be those who will criticize your purpose. There will always be those who speak about what you are doing, how you are doing it, and talk about why you are doing it. Some people will never be satisfied with you. There will not be any other reason except you are their focus and guess what that is none of your business. You read it right sis, the issues with you are none of your business. There is a song called "None of My Business" by Christian artist Andy Mineo. He speaks about how it is not his business what "they" think about him! The point is if you are focused on your purpose then you have no time to worry about "them". This is the day where you are no longer concerned about those chatterboxes around you. This season you are laser-focused on your assignment at hand. Move on passed the talkers, go ahead and give them something to talk about.

We know the story of Noah in the bible in Genesis chapters 6 and 7, God gave Noah an instruction that made no sense to humanity at all. He told this man to build an ark, a large boat, because the world is about to flood. Now listen, I do not know about you, but I am not sure how I would have responded to this instruction. Remember that it had never rained on the earth. So, the thought of completing an instruction totally out of the box amid the naysayers probably seemed a little insane. It was enough to receive the word from God, but it takes another level of boldness to trust the voice of God within you when there are those around you that are secretly laughing or openly laughing at your faith moves. It is not easy to continue when you have everyone second guessing your actions. I have been there my sister. God has asked me to build and to create projects that I have never seen before or heard of in my life. There were no road maps, there were no blueprints and there were no role models that accompanied the instructions. All I could lean on was God and a Word! Whew, that will preach.

You will have to build on your foundation and history with God; (your trust in God) and a Word. Are you willing to look crazy or foolish in the moment knowing that you heard from God? I can tell you that anyone that is daring to do something extraordinary, will at some point question am I crazy or am I in faith? Just think about the result of your obedience, you will not look crazy when you are walking into that bank cashing or depositing a million-dollar check. You will not because you chose to believe that God had something more in store for you. Your audacity in faith will yield results, just keep going. You are not crazy sis; you are in faith!

Who had the last laugh in Noah's situation? They mocked him, scoffed at him, talked about him. People will come to the construction site of your building and tell you to your face that you are crazy and that it will never work. I have a word from the Lord for you, keep building sis! When "they" remind you that you are a single mom, you keep going to school to get the degree. When they remind you of how broke you are, you continue making the business plan and sowing your seed, because the money will come.

When they remind you of your past, then you keep speaking about your future. I do not care how many people tell you that you cannot, or you should not, you remember to keep building! You will only look crazy for a minute, but you will have a lifetime of giving God all the glory because of your BIG FAITH!

Let your legacy be that she dared to believe God. Let them say, "Wow, That Woman did it!!"

You are well on your way. You are not alone. You are extraordinary, you are powerful, you are a woman of destiny and purpose. You are bold and fierce and full of potential.

I want you to take a moment to write down the crazy ideas and dreams that you see when you close your eyes. Not the safe, easy dream, I want you to take the time to write down what you are afraid to believe and write it down in living color. Write that thing that is too big for you. Pull up some audacity and just take the first step and write it down. Sometimes the first step is just to write it down. Habakkuk 2 says to write the vision and make it plain. I dare you to write it down. Get it out of your head. I double-dog dare you to just take the step to write it and let's see what God will do with it. I am so excited about this step of faith!

1._____

2._____

3._____

4._____

5._____

6._____

Great job! I am supporting you sis and remember that I am in your fan club now! You have someone who is rooting for you and who believes that you can accomplish everything that God has ordained for you to do on this earth. Let's Go!

Can You DO THIS? AND OUR ANSWER IS,

Girl, YES YOU CAN!!!!

CHAPTER

8

YOU ARE ALREADY VALIDATED BY GOD!

Likes are Nice, But not Necessary Already Approved!

#8
"You are already Validated by God! Likes are Nice, But not Necessary. Already Approved!

Good morning Royal Daughter. That is right you are royalty, and you should be addressed as such. Come on let's be real ladies most of us didn't grow up in a royal castle with maidservants taking care of our every need. We were not fed with a silver spoon in our mouths, but that does not mean that we cannot live like we are of royal blood. I have been sent into this earth to remind you, and to inform some of you, that you are of royal descent. You are a daughter of God, and you have access to his absolute best simply because you belong to him. Now let's get started with this day. It is time to meet purpose head-on.

It took me a while to believe this quote today. We live in such a social media-saturated world. The need for likes, hearts, shares, and comments have allowed such a delusion of validation and approval from people that we do not even know. There is a new trend now that people can become Tik Tok Famous or go viral. That was never heard of when I was growing up. It took hard work and a serious grind to become famous. That investment took place so that it meant something of value. Now in today's culture anyone without credibility can become famous and get a platform. Side Note: Some people on social media work hard! People are viral and yet in the culture today suicides are on the rise, addictive lifestyles of alcohol and drugs are higher than ever. Depression and eating disorders are more prevalent now than ever in history because of what the trend has dictated and set a precedence that likes, and hearts are the "new" definition of approval.

I feel so saddened by so many young women that compare themselves to other women. Many young ladies feel like they fall short in the way that they look or the way that their bodies are shaped or even how they speak. This generation feels the need to compare their worthiness to the amount of money that they make. So many are, "Chasing the Bag!" Why do we need the approval of people when we know that we have already been validated by God?

Jeremiah 1:5 KJV
[5] Before I formed thee in the belly, I knew thee, and before thou camest forth out of the womb I sanctified thee, and I ordained thee a prophet unto the nations....

I love this verse because God spoke to Jeremiah the prophet and reminded him of when he began his approval and validation. The verse said before he came out of his mother's womb, the Lord already sanctified and ordained him. His calling and purpose were already established and did not need the approval of man for activation before he walked in it. I love what my husband says, "God made you because there was a purpose that needed to be fulfilled in the earth realm, not the other way around". Your purpose was already established, stamped, marked, approved, and validated before you were even born. Wow that is a word.

Sis, so how can you sit around and compare yourself to anyone else's purpose or destiny? Your calling was tailor-made just for you. Your calling fits you perfectly. God knew how to make your purpose just for you. That is why you cannot fit into doing something that was not designed for you. You will not ever be fulfilled trying to wear someone else's call or purpose. You wonder why you look different, sound different, sing different, approach things differently, because it was on purpose.

God did not make a mistake. The enemy wants you to get caught up and distracted by waiting on people to approve your moves. I finally understood that some people may not ever approve or validate what it is that I am called to do and guess what? It is ok.

I believe that we hold people hostage to what we think we know. It is such a restrictive limitation when we try to shove people into molds that are man-made. It is unfair to their potential and their destiny. Many times, we criticize what we do not understand instead of inquiring or praying about what we have yet to be exposed to. With all that said, seek the Lord diligently about who you are and what you are called to do. Get under proper leadership, covering, and accountability to help guide your journey to destiny. I believe there is safety in accountability. But I also encourage you to be your WHOLE AUTHENTIC self sis! Do not wait, move today! You may never receive approval or validation from anyone that you are looking to. Remember that God has already ordained you because you were formed and born into the world for your purpose. Validation was initiated by your birth. That is proof!

Okay, it is time to do the work. What have you been hiding from? Have you been waiting on someone's approval or validation? What can you do today to begin to move towards what God has asked you to do? Even if there is not a following of people or a support team, I encourage you to do it anyway? Make your move today. Name the areas that have laid dormant in your life. Say this statement out loud...

"I will no longer hide or lay dormant in the following area....

a._____

b._____

c._____

d._____

e._____

f._____

Lord, I pray for my sister today as she names the areas that she is taking off the shelf, the areas that she is bringing out of hiding. I pray for the boldness, the courage, and the wisdom of the Lord over her as she trusts you. It can be scary to step out in faith, but I thank you that as she acknowledges you in all her ways that you will surely direct her path. Her steps are ordered of you, and I pray that pleasing you will be at the top of her priority list. Bless her in her endeavors and bring her to great success to you!

CHAPTER

9

KNOW YOUR LIMITATIONS AND YOUR VALUE

Pour and Serve Responsibly from your OVERFLOW!

#9
Know Your Limitations and Your Value.
Pour and Serve Responsibly from your OVERFLOW!

Hey, my beautiful sister! How are you feeling on this wonderful day? I pray that your life is in full motion of purpose and destiny! No more delay, please do not wait. Girl, there is a whole world waiting on you to get up and shake things up. You may be thinking, how can little ole' me shake up anything? Well, I am here to inform you that you underestimate what you carry. Woman, there is a spiritual well that is so deep within you, and it carries fresh water and treasures that the world needs. We change this world by each person's obedience. So, go ahead and get up and get dressed for success today!

This quote is so crucially important to every woman. Women that have responsibilities are such hard workers. The numerous amounts of hats we wear can be stressful and overwhelming but somehow by God's grace, we find a way to continue to nurture and care for those that we have been called to steward. Our husbands, children, family members, job responsibility, financial responsibilities, our homes, our churches, and mentees, all drink from our cups. We pour something of ourselves into each of the categories in our lives and yet for some reason, self-care, mental health, our well-being is usually put on the back burner and then we wonder why we soon burn out. The result of no self-care ends in a crash or a blow-up because we are on empty and have not stopped to refill our tanks.

I teach the women that I have had the honor to train and mentor, that it is irresponsible of you to give what you do not have. It is honestly arrogant to think that you never need a refilling. It is not healthy to think of yourself as this superwoman that is invincible and to never allow yourself the outlet to get poured into. Who is pouring into you? Who is taking care of you today? When do you receive a moment to breathe? When was the last time you took yourself to the spa or to get your nails done? When was the last time you flew out to a women's retreat to get revitalized and strengthened? Preachers, Pastors, and Ministers, who are you sitting under? Who is feeding you the WORD? This is a part of the accountability structure that I spoke about in the last chapter. You cannot pour from an empty cistern. When you are full, then you can pour, and you have something left over to live on.

Let's discuss walking into an overflow. When your cistern is spilling over the sides of your cup, the vessel does not have to move. It is not necessary to pick it up and pour, people can just come to where you are and receive of that which is spilling over on them. Less effort is made when there is an overflow in your life. When there is a faucet that is constantly pouring into an already full vessel, then every person is being taken care of. There is the flow from your faucet, and you are being filled while everyone around you is receiving the overflow of your vessel. So, when the Lord asks you to pour into another vessel, then you will have more than enough to give out into other vessels without the threat of becoming empty. What am I saying? Keep a faucet pouring into YOU! This is so important women of God.

I pray this is hitting you where it initiates a priority shift. I wrote all of that to say, that you must walk into a season of unapologetically receiving. This was such a hard concept for me to walk into. I had no issue with giving and pouring out of my substance, but when it was time for me to receive, I would put a lid on my cistern and think that I was doing mankind or those around me some good. What a backwards way of thinking. I was robbing everyone around me of my best self. I did not realize that I was operating in place of self-sabotage. I was operating in a thwarted way of thinking. It was really a poverty mentality that was active in my life, and I paid dearly for it, and everyone else around me paid for it as well.

I noticed that I had been operating below my best self. When I finally allowed God to bring people into my life to pour into me then I became so much more pleasant to be around. I was less resentful in thinking that everyone was taking from me instead of pouring into me. Wow, many tried to pour into my life, but I was operating in such a backwards mentality and rejecting the very life and sustaining strength that I desperately needed. To look back, I missed out on so many opportunities to be ministered to. Your maintenance, your infilling, your cultivation is so critical to your purpose and to those that you are called to.

During the 2020 quarantine and pandemic, I was forced to submit to God. He forced me to sit down and take a self-inventory of where I was located. He let me know that if I was to successfully grab purpose then I cannot microwave past self-work.

So as a result of this submission I started therapy, I began to take care of my body with exercise and eating healthy, and I began to explore activities and hobbies that I love. I did not realize that I had a love for painting, and I am fairly good at it. I found that painting is a safe space for me to clear my head through creativity while creating something so beautiful. Girl let's be real, I'm not Michael Angelo or anything, but my home is more beautiful because of my newfound hobby. After these few changes, I began to fill full of life, I developed more energy and vigor. I began to look forward to the next day with joy instead of approaching my days with disdain and stress.

Action Plan:

What can you do today that will facilitate the area of overflow in your life? Where are you empty? What small step can you take right now that will refuel your life to become the best version of yourself? Remember people are waiting for the overflow in your life.

1._____   2. _____

3._____   4. _____

5._____   6. _____

7._____   8. _____

CHAPTER

10

YOUR SEASON IS ABOUT TO CHANGE, IT'S YOUR SEASON TO PROSPER

Schedule your success through Movement!

10

Your Season is about to change, It is Your Season to Prosper. Schedule your success through Movement.

Hello, Woman of Authority. Yes you, I am talking to you. You were called to have dominion and to rule in your sphere of authority. You have been commissioned to operate in full authority in the area where you have been given rulership. That authority is to be used whether that is in your home, on your job, in your family, your church, or over yourself.
Whatever sphere you have been afforded, make sure that you show up today in full authority with your head up sis, and knowing that your confidence is in the Lord.

I want to take the time to encourage those who have been in a low place for a long time. Life can be tough and when believing God for better, sometimes it seems as if things get worse before they get better. Life can throw blow after blow after blow after blow and many times will not allow you enough time to breathe between blows. Can I get a witness? Girl, if I could tell you of the seasons of being in Lodebar. (2 Samuel 9) Lodebar was a city named in 2 Samuel chapter 9. A man name Mephibosheth lived there, and this place was considered the lowest of the low. It was a place where people were forgotten, ostracized, casted away to never be remembered. It was a lonely place that did not have much life. There were not many green pastures or grass or flowers there. It was not a place that anyone wanted to be a part of. This was known as the wrong side of the tracks.

68

I love this story because Mephibosheth probably thought that he was forgotten. He was the son of his late father Johnathan, King David's most beloved friend in the world. Because of Johnathan's loyalty, love, and obedience to God and to his friend David, he ultimately scheduled success for his son and his grandson. He did not understand that his movements during his lifetime scheduled success for his legacy that transferred to his son and grandson.

Mephibosheth went from the lowest in the kingdom to eating at the King's table for the rest of his days. Not only did he inherit the best meals, but he also inherited all the real estate that his grandfather King Saul owned, and he inherited servants to take care of his estate all the days of his life. Sis, I am getting excited sitting here typing at this computer. I bind the enemy who comes at night and during your days to discourage you and to tell you that your work is in vain. I bind the enemy who spews lies to you to make you think that your obedience is in vain, and that it will never make a difference or yield any harvest. Baby, listen, as long as the sun remains there is a principle of seedtime and harvest. Your obedience to God will always yield a reward!

You are about to come into a season of great success this season. Wow, I feel an anointing on this quote today. Your seasons of not having enough are coming to an end. Many of you have been laboring in the vineyard and have been asking God, when is it my turn? When will I see the light of day? When will my lonely days be over? When will I get a break, God? Your obedience has opened a door to your new season of breakthrough. Hold on, just a little while longer sister! Here grab ahold of my faith in the spirit realm. Let me hold you up a little bit with my faith. You cannot let go now. That devil has lied to you long enough and told you that it is not working. HA, honey, it is more than working, it is about to cause you to walk into a realm that you never thought possible. You are about to experience a paradigm shift. A paradigm is defined by Google- paradigm (par··dīm'), n a **generally accepted model for making sense of phenomena in a given discipline at a particular time**. When one paradigm is replaced by another, it is called a paradigm shift.

You once accepted the paradigm of your current life of trauma, dysfunction, and poverty (mind, emotional or financial), but let me tell you something Woman of God, God is about to replace your old paradigm with a completely new one. As the definition read, you will now have to explain this phenomenon that God is working on right now. Jesus! I do not want to preach today, but people will wonder HOW?!!! How in the world were you broke one day and now you are rich? Somebody needs to shout right there. How is it one day you were in the middle of a nervous breakdown and now you are in full clarity of mind? How is it that you were crying tears of torment yesterday and today you are laughing with bouts of joy? How is it that you were homeless yesterday and today you are now a homeowner?

Sis, I want you to pick yourself up from your bed, couch, or floor wherever you are and begin to decree over your life what God said to you. I love the song "Never Lost a Battle" by All Nations Worship Assembly.

The song speaks, the dark cannot whisper away what God said to you in the light. My God during your night season many voices will come to tell you that there is no hope and that you are crazy for believing that there could ever be something other than what you see. We are here to dismantle all of those lies. You are about to embark on a new life, a new journey in this season. Sis you must believe that it is working for your good. Things will get better! God has not forgotten about you.

Psalms 30:5b - Weeping may endure for a night but joy comes in the morning light.

Sis, I need you to believe God, do not give up. Listen to me, this too shall pass.

Ephesians 3:20 20Now to him who can **do** immeasurably more than **all we ask or** imagine, according to his power that is at work within us,

Now, today's Action Plan is as follows. I want you to take the next page and write your confession of faith. This confession is what you want to see and of course, you must include the scriptures that will back up what you say. I know many times we do not want to write things out or to take the time to invest in ourselves. Remember this will working on your overflow from the last chapter. It is time for a paradigm shift in your mind and you must change and renew your mind in the Word of God. So, let's go and get started! Begin writing!

My Confession of Faith/My Prophetic Declaration

CHAPTER

11

POSITIONING AND ALIGNMENT ARE KEY IN THIS SEASON

Set yourself up
for your next!
Get Ready!

#11

Positioning and Alignment are Key in this season. Set yourself up for your next! Get Ready!

Good morning my Sista, Queen of your domain! How are you this morning royal daughter? Go ahead and get used to that type of language. Why would I say that? It is how God sees you and I have learned that I must position myself around people who speak highly of me as well. I must think good thoughts of myself. Sidenote: I am not saying that people need to go around calling you queen all the time. I am saying to surround yourself with people who value you. It makes such a difference in your world. Before you receive words of affirmation from anyone else, speak those kinds of words to yourself! Do not wait on others to do it first. You speak!

This quote today is so vital for you. It is necessary for your manifestation of the promises of God in your life.

The word position is to put or arrange (someone or something) in a particular place or way. The word alignment is defined as a position of agreement or alliance. Both words are critical to your success.

When you position yourself, you get into the correct placement to receive. You are in the correct posture and in anticipation of what you are preparing for. Many times, we can miss opportunities and great doors because we were in the wrong posture. For instance, God says that you are a leader and when He opens a

74

great opportunity for you to step into that place, if you are not positioned in the proper place then you are not ready to receive. This could be because you are hiding in depression or low self-worth. Maybe you are postured in self-pity and lacking in confidence. I am not throwing stones or shade queen; I am speaking from experience. I have been there and have missed some prime-time opportunities in my life. I promise you I will not miss anymore, and I am telling you this, so you will not miss any either. I have received the scars and wounds of being out of position during my seasons of elevation, so you do not have to miss yours.

One of the prayers that I pray on a regular basis is from: **1 Chronicle 12:32** It reads, "³²And of the children **of Issachar**, which were men that had an understanding of **the times....**

I pray this prayer of discerning the times and seasons because I understand the devastation of missing the timing of God. I once heard a quote that states, "procrastination is the arrogant thought that God owes you another opportunity to do what you have time to do today." It is so true; it is so easy to procrastinate, however ladies we are in position in this season so that God can fulfill His promises concerning us. God is saying today, get in your rightful place. Your blessings are here, your peace is here, your resources are here. Come out of hiding and stand in your rightful place. This is the time and season to walk into your identity.

Alignment is such a powerful word. This word is so powerful because it works hand in hand with your agreement. What are you aligned with in this season? Who are you in alignment with? God honors agreement. He said where two or three are touching and agreeing on anything, then he would be there in the midst. God also honors alignment. Something powerful happens when there is alignment and when there is a proper agreement! My God that will preach! However, the devil loves agreement as well. He sows seeds of damnation, seeds of discouragement, seeds of inferiority, and what he wants from you is your agreement. He cannot do anything without your alignment. I love to reference Joyce Meyer's book, one of my favorite long-distanced mentors, the "Battlefield Is in the Mind". If the enemy can form an alliance with you in your mind, then he can control your outcome!! How you see yourself will determine your destiny.

So, the question is who are you in alignment with and are you in a position for the move of God in your life? This is an immensely powerful equation and formula. Today I want you to stop and think about your position and your alignment. The two together speaks volumes that you are ready for your next. This formula will notify heaven that you are serious about getting what belongs to you. I decree and declare that you are a woman that no longer underestimates her position on this earth. You are no longer a woman who underestimates the power of her alliance! I pray that you are deciding today to get up and change your posture and to change your mind.

You know what time it is. It is time for our "Action Plan". We know that faith without works is dead! What has been your position and posture in the last year? Have you heard the voice of God concerning your future and did you run the other way? What can you do today to position yourself? What do you need to come out of alignment with, and what do you need to come into agreement with? You know how we do these ladies, let's write this down right now!!

Action Plan! (Be Honest and Open)

CHAPTER

12

KEEP GOING, I KNOW IT DOESN'T FEEL LIKE IT'S WORKING

Sis,
You are Gaining
Momentum!

#12

"Keep going, I know it doesn't feel like it's working, But Sis, it's working for You."

Good morning Daughter of Zion, Princess of God's heart. Wow, what an honor to be called a daughter of God. I value that position more than any other position or title that could ever be given to me. You are so important and loved by the creator of the universe. You are the apple of God's eye. How do you know that Katria? Well, I know it because he loved us so much to give his only son Jesus to make a way for me to be with him. Who else would sacrifice their only Son for you? If you have ever questioned how much you are loved, just remember what God has already done for you! So, with that amazing thought in mind, let's get started in this day of purpose,

This quote today is one of great encouragement. I will be honest ladies, most of us are out here trying to make the world go around as my husband would say. We are hard workers. We wear a multiplicity of hats. We are wives, mothers, babysitters, financial advisors, entrepreneurs, teachers, lawyers, doctors, pastors, and every position that you can think of. While working to accomplish a dream while simultaneously working to make a successful family life, you may come to a point where it seems as if you are not making much progress. It is frustrating to feel that your wheels are spinning around in the mud. We all have been there in life; so, sis you are not alone.

No matter what path you are on today and have been on in this last season, just remember that your payoff will eventually come. I love the song by the Christian group, Mary, Mary, this song speaks that you cannot give up now. You must realize that you have come too far to stop now. I love that song because it references how sometimes you just feel like throwing in the towel, but then you realize that you have come to far to give up. Come on can I get a witness on this page right now. May I have a transparent moment? There have been times when I have started a project and felt during the process that this is not working. There are moments where I asked God, are you sure? Am I even doing the right thing? Am I wasting my time?

Sis, I am here today to tell you that you are gaining more ground than you think. You are not losing like you think you are. Even in failure, there is so much to be gained! At least you walk away with greater knowledge and understanding of what not to do next time. You are smarter because of the mistakes. Your perspective is everything girlfriend. Friend, you are well on your way to greatness. God loves to reward diligence. The bible speaks in Hebrews 11:6b....and that He is a rewarder of them that diligently seek Him. This verse says that if you keep seeking after God there is a reward for those that do not quit. There is your word, do not quit today or any day!

You are not a quitter; it is not in your make-up. You are meant to finish strong! I pray that God would reveal to you today of how far you have come. Sometimes we can be so busy with working that we do not take the time out to stop to see how far God has brought us. You must stop to celebrate what you have accomplished. You may not be on the mountain top yet, but you sure have worked to get out of the valley, and I am so proud of you girl! You betta work! Yes, I know how to spell betta, but I meant to say BETTA!! You BETTA WORK MY SIS!!

Here is a reminder to you on this journey while working, you must remember that someone is always watching you. It would be nice to live this life incognito, however that is just wishful thinking. I believe God set up life like that on purpose. He knew that we would need to take detours off the straight path to pick up another sister or brother on the way to our destination. How you endure your journey can make or break someone's decision to keep it moving. There was a season in my life where God would allow women from different places to comment, whether on social media or in person, on something that they saw about me. These observations happened when I did not think anyone was looking at me. They would speak so highly of my journey and would speak on the grace and dignity that I walked in while going through utter HELL. Ha, I chuckle because as I think back over those seasons, in those moments I felt so discouraged. I felt like I was falling apart from the seams. I felt lost and I needed a clue, but the grace of God covered me. I did not realize that even though I felt like crap, they saw the greater parts of me! God's grace covered me. Wow, what a notion! I was gaining more ground than I knew. God had forged attributes of endurance, and determination and so many other character traits that shined greater than the dark place I was located in. Jesus, I am so grateful that God did not give up on me. Daughter of Zion, I am here to remind you that He is not giving up on you either. I am not giving up on you and you will not give up on yourself. I decree and declare that you will not quit! You will finish this race that is set before you. I know it has been hard, and I know that you are tired, but dry your eyes and keep going! Take your moment to reset and then get up. You are gaining more than you are losing. You will get there and remember I am here cheering you on!

Action plan......

You know what time it is Queen, Faith without works is dead! We are not only hearers, but we are doers of the word! Let's Go!!

Today encourage yourself in the Lord:

_____
_____
_____
_____
_____
_____
_____
_____
_____
_____
_____
_____
_____
_____
_____
_____
_____
_____
_____
_____

CHAPTER

13

"VICTORY LAP"

Just keep
moving!
Run Your Race
at God's Pace
For you!

#13
Victory Lap!
Just keep moving! Run Your Race at God's Pace
For you!

Good morning Queen. How are you today? I pray that you wake up feeling like the royalty you are! I want to end this book on a note of MEGA encouragement to you as you continue every day in purpose. It is easy to despise your current location because of the zeal to get to another destination in your journey. Today, get up and focus on being content with who you are, where you are and where you are going! I did not say be satisfied. I know that sounds foreign to some, however you must remember that today's purpose is just as important to your destiny as tomorrow's destination. You do not want to miss one moment of the time you are given in any day trying to make it somewhere into the future. Go out today and smell the roses. Go out today and take a walk by a lake or even play with your kids at the playground. You will get to your destiny; however, your purpose is awaiting you on today.

Today's quote is so powerful. Do not despise crawling or even limping. Wow, what a notion right? Society says that the sprinter, those who run at a faster pace are considered successful. However, I differ in opinion on this one. Just because someone makes it to their finish line quicker does not make them any better or more successful. Do not compare your beginning to someone's finish. Did you hear me woman of God? Do not compare yourself to anyone.

Do you remember the childhood nursery story of the tortoise and the hare? The hare (rabbit) mocked the tortoise (turtle) because of his slow movement. However, the turtle did not let the mockery distract him. He was so confident in his ability that he challenged the hare to a race. Now in natural logic, this seems ridiculous, but you must be confident in what you bring to the table. God knew what He was doing when He chose you to do your purpose. The hare was so arrogant that he was better and would win that he began to slack on his race and decided to take a nap. The tortoise stayed the course slow and steady and passed the sleeping hare on to win the race. The moral of the story is the race is not given to the swift, but to the one who endures till the end.

Another problem with the rabbit is that there was a comparison of what he could do faster. The rabbit operated in pride. Pride will get you nowhere but out of the race. James 4:6 says that "God resists the pride but gives grace to the humble". My mother has always taught me that the quickest way up is to go down. In other words, stay humble women of God. In this season when God begins to elevate you remember to stay in a low place of humility. That is the quickest way to be elevated. Get low and stay low and as you rise remember to give God all the glory! You are about to reach heights unknown with this attitude of humility.

The turtle had something great. He focused on his strengths, and he stayed in his lane. He did not speed up to match the hare. He did not try a different strategy to try to match his competitor, he simply stayed with what he knew he did well. He was crawling in comparison to his competition, but he won the race. What is the moral of this story? I believe that there are several themes here

1. You do not have to be the quickest to win the race. Everyone has their own race to run. You want God to say, "Well done"!
2. Do not compare your skills, talents, or gifts with anyone else. You are uniquely created on purpose for purpose. Sis, we need what you have to offer.
3. Do not underestimate your strengths. What you carry is enough. What you have is what you need. YOU ARE ENOUGH!
4. Stay the course, even if it seems like you are behind. Even if you are last, you do not stop until you cross over the finish line. Remember someone is watching you.
5. Stay humble and focus on your strengths and avoid distractions. In this season get a laser-focus and move in your lane. You shine best when you are in your own lane.

Action Plan:

LIVE, LIVE,   LIVE, LIVE!!
ON PURPOSE

About the Author

Pastor Katria Bell is first, a daughter of God, wife of 25 years to Troy Bell Sr., and mother of 6 + bonus daughter in Love! She is also Senior Pastor at Ignite Church Tulsa, in Tulsa, OK along with her husband.

Pastor Katria Bell is an Apostolic Prophet called to the 5-fold ministry. She is a published Author, the Visionary of God's Butterflies Ministries (Women's Empowerment and Training), an Entrepreneur, Host of Living on Purpose Moments Webisodes (Facebook and Instagram) weekly, the Director of "Finding Y.O.U" (Women's Mentorship Program), a Mentor, Trainer, and Spiritual Mother. She is called to train and disciple leaders for the Kingdom of God.

Pastor Katria is the author of the books God's Butterflies-A Woman's Journey Through Transformation, Project manager and Co-Author of The Grace Under Fire Series, and the author of the New Release- "Girl, Yes You Can!" all available on www.katriabellministries.org, Amazon.com, Barnes and Noble, and Audible Platforms.

GOD'S BUTTERFLIES- Women's Empowerment
Pastor Katria has been mantled to carry the heartbeat of God to his daughters in what she calls the "Butterfly Experience". This is a life changing encounter where women are carried away and catered to in an intimate experience with God. These women are whisked away for 1-2 days and showered with gifts, they are celebrated at a personal ceremony with only close family and friends, and then ushered into one-on-one ministry impartation in what is called the "UPPER ROOM EXPERIENCE". This Prophetic Encounter is one that revolutionizes their intimate relationship with God. You simply must experience the "Hot Seat" to understand this life changing event.

My Sister's Keeper was developed from the God's Butterflies Journey to provide a monthly local meeting in Tulsa, OK, referred to as the "Safe Place". This is a monthly event for women to worship together, fellowship in small group settings, to receive the Word of God and break bread in a safe haven.

Pastor Katria also mentors, trains, and is a Spiritual Mother to Women of God across the Nation. She also developed the "Finding You Challenge", a mentorship program to help women identify who they are and gives direction and guidance to embrace their God-given identity. This growth track produces practical and spiritual steps to help women live out their purpose in the earth. Y.O.U. stands for Yielded, Overcoming, and Upgraded Women.

Journaling

FLY BUTTERFLIES, FLY!!!!!

_____

_____

_____

_____

_____

_____

_____

_____

_____

_____

_____

_____

_____

_____

_____

_____

GIRL, I DECREE

AND DECLARE

THAT THIS IS

YOUR

BREAK-OUT

SEASON!

GIRL, I DECREE

AND DECLARE

THAT YOU

WILL WALK

IN UNUSUAL

FAVOR THIS

YEAR!

GIRL,

I DECREE

AND DECLARE

THAT NO

WEAPON

FORMED

AGAINST YOU

WILL PROSPER!
GIRL,

I DECREE AND

DECLARE

THAT YOU

WILL LIVE

AND EXPERIENCE

YOUR

BIG DREAMS!

GIRL,

I DECREE AND DECLARE OVER YOUR LIFE SUPERNATURAL BLESSINGS AND BREAKTHROUGH!

SIS, I DECREE

AND DECLARE

OVER YOUR

LIFE THAT

FEAR IS

DEFEATED, YOU

WILL WALK IN

BOLDNESS!!

GIRL,

YOU

ARE

ABSOLUTELY

GORGEOUS,

INSIDE AND OUT!

SIS,

HOLD

YOUR

HEAD UP!

WALK WITH A

FIERCE

UNAPOLOGETIC

ANOINTING!

SIS,

DO NOT

WAIT ON

PEOPLE'S

APPROVAL

YOU HAVE

ALREADY BEEN

VALIDATED!

GIRL,

REMEMBER

YES YOU CAN!!

PLEASE SUBMIT

A REVIEW ON

AMAZON.COM

AND FIND MORE TITLES

ON

WWW.KATT___LAHNISTI__ES.ORG

OTHER TITLES:

GOD'S BUTTERFLIES- A WOMAN'S
JOURNEY THROUGH TRANSFORMATION

GRACE UNDER FIRE

GIRL, YES YOU CAN

UPCOMING PROJECTS:

GRACE UNDER FIRE- PART 2
RELATIONSHIP SERIES

WOMAN IN THE MIDDLE

WORK CITED PAGE

"Theodore Roosevelt Quotes". OSMQuote.com,
https://www.OSMQuote.com/quote/theodore-roosevelt-quote-528e0b, accessed March 15, 2020.

Made in the USA
Coppell, TX
28 December 2021